Introd

Here are twenty routes to explore
of the Brecon Beacons National F
hidden woodland dells, astoundir
All twenty walks are 'mini-adventures' c
majestic national park.

The Park stretches for 50 miles from east to west. In the west, the Black Mountains present a dramatic high escarpment along the English border straddled by Offa's Dyke long distance path. A succession of deep, wooded valleys dissects the mountain range, bringing fast flowing streams from the waterlogged moorland to the Usk and Wye river systems. Monks and farmers have shared these lands, their legacy most notably seen at the haunting remains of Llanthony Priory in the Honddu Valley.

In the centre of the Park lie the highest peaks of the region, the loftiest, Pen y Fan, only just failing to make the 'Munro' height of 3000 feet. The characteristic sandstone caps of the summits bring an iconic profile to the ridge south of Brecon.

To the west lie the lonely, exposed uplands of Fforest Fawr and the Black Mountain. Bannau Brycheinog and Bannau Sir Gaer combine to draw a dramatic and distinctive skyline above the source of the Usk. While in the south, the limestone underbelly of the Park is exposed to create a fascinating landscape of woodland and waterfalls, caves and caverns.

There are many nooks and crannies to explore throughout the National Park. This series of walks explores many of these. Some use waymarked trails, others combine picturesque paths or open moorland. All are easy to follow.

Although these are short walks, there is no shortage of excitement, challenge and variety. A number of walks discover nature reserves and wildlife hotspots, such as Pwll-y-Wrach (Walk 2) or Coed-y-Cerrig (Walk 9). Others explore forests, including Taf Fechan (Walk 13) and Mynydd Ddu (Walk 10). There are plenty of chances to visit historic sites like Carreg Cennen Castle (Walk 19) or the mysterious Iron Age remains on nearby Garn Goch (Walk 18). Some walks give the chance to conquer the highest ground of the Beacons like Hay Bluff (Walk 1) or the Sugar Loaf (Walk 11). Water is a common theme from the reservoirs in Walks 14 and 20 to the historic Monmouthshire & Brecon Canal in Walks 5 and 12.

If you also like longer walks there are two sister volumes published by Kittiwake, covering the eastern section of the park (*Walking in the Black Mountains*) and the central and western areas (*Walking in the Brecon Beacons*). These books include a total of 40 longer walks and mountain expeditions. Walks 4, 6, 7 and 14 are revised versions of walks published in an earlier guide to the Brecon Beacons; all the other walks are entirely new.

All outdoor activity requires some care. Some walks include sections on high, exposed moorland. In these cases, go properly equipped with appropriate clothing and navigational equipment. There are endless opportunities to discover new places and renew your spirit across the Beacons. Here are twenty places and walks to enjoy.

HAY BLUFF

DESCRIPTION An exhilarating taster of the wild moorland of the Black Mountains, with panoramic views from the edge of the plateau.

DISTANCE & TERRAIN 2½ miles. A short but steep climb gains the summit of Hay Bluff before traversing the moorland interior of the plateau. The return route rakes down the side of the ridge with splendid views throughout. Although this is a short walk on good paths, it crosses wild and remote country and you will need mountain clothing and footwear.

START Roadside parking area one mile north of Gospel Pass, the summit of the mountain road between Hay and Llanthony. SO 239373.

DIRECTIONS From Hay town centre take B4350 towards Brecon for a few hundred yards. When this bends right, turn sharp left to follow a minor road, signposted to Capel-y-ffin. This is the mountain road that crosses the Black Mountains to Llanthony and Abergavenny. Continue along this for about 3 miles, climbing steadily, until you reach an extensive open grassy plateau next to a road junction, just below the ridge of the mountains. There is a small parking area here, right beneath the summit of Hay Bluff.

I *From the start the views are panoramic. To the north, border country spreads out at your feet, from the Clee Hills of Shropshire to the Radnor Hills of Mid Wales. Westwards the distant profile of the Brecon Beacons guards the route into the hinterland of Wales.* Leave the road between the parking area and the adjacent road junction, taking a broad grassy clearing between the gorse bushes, heading directly for the summit of Hay Bluff. Initially gentle, the gradient soon becomes steeper. In about ¼ of a mile, about half way up, bear right at a junction of paths and continue ascending, now diagonally across the face of the mountain. After a further ¼ of a mile, arrive abruptly at the top, on the edge of the plateau. Turn left, walking along the edge of the escarpment, to reach the trig point at the top of Hay Bluff.

2 *At over 2000 feet (667m), Hay Bluff's altitude alone would qualify it as a mountain. However, from the summit it is evident that its impressive northern profile is indeed a bluff, as the trig point simply marks the terminal elevation of a vast area of lofty moorland. As the trig point rises a mere 35 feet above the lowest point of this moorland, it fails to gain mountain status. None of these statistical technicalities diminish Hay Bluff's theatrical position or airy vantage point one whit. Like the bow of a ship, it strains north from the moorland plateau, providing imperious oversight across the Wye valley. From far to the east, its emphatic silhouette marks is out as the first sentinel of mountainous Wales.* At the trig point, turn right to take a level surfaced path across heather moorland. *To the right, look across the ridges of the Black Mountains, spreading west like the fingers of a hand. Immediately to the right, the upper reaches of the Honddu Valley cut a trench through the wild uplands, carrying the mountain road down to Capel-y-ffyn. The ridge beyond includes Waun Fach, the highest point of the Black Mountains. Further west are the summits of the Brecon Beacons.*

3 In about ½ a mile from Hay Bluff, come to a junction of paths, just before a short, rocky rise. The junction is marked by a small stone Offa's Dyke marker. Turn sharp left here, almost doubling back, and follow the stone causeway path on the route of the Long Distance Path. *There are now views northwards across the undulating farmland of Herefordshire and Shropshire and the path soon begins to descend, overlooking the head of the Monnow Valley to the right.* A well surfaced route then rakes down the side of the ridge. Lower down it becomes grassy, crossing areas of gorse and bracken, eventually reaching a boggy area towards the bottom. Offa's Dyke Path continues ahead at this point to reach the road in less than ¼ mile. However, you can turn left here to find a grassy passage through the bracken to take you directly back to the parking area.

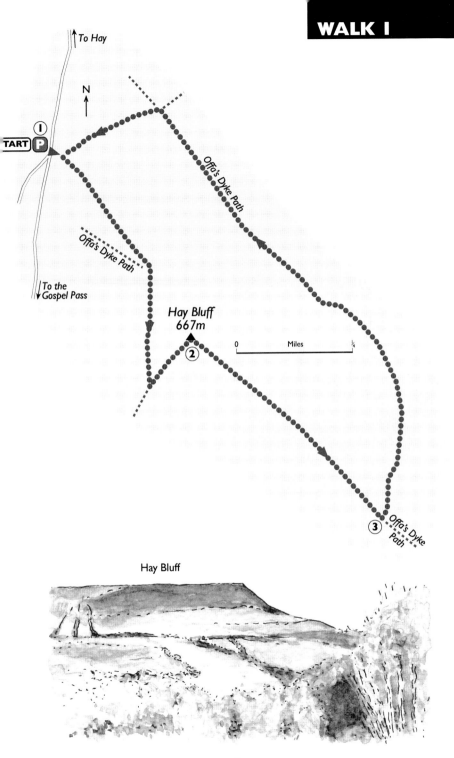

To Hay

N

START

To the
Gospel Pass

Offa's Dyke Path

Offa's Dyke Path

Hay Bluff
667m

Offa's Dyke
Path

0   Miles   ¼

Hay Bluff

THE WITCH'S POOL

DESCRIPTION A short walk around a woodland nature reserve, clinging to the steep sided valley of the River Enig. At the far end, the river cascades down a spectacular waterfall. Pwll-y-Wrach means, 'The Witch's Pool'. Whatever the origin of the name, it is certainly a hidden and enchanting valley.

DISTANCE AND TERRAIN 1½ miles with longer or shorter alternatives. This is an easy walk but there is one quite steep descent and the paths can be muddy and slippery. The all-ability walkway offers a shorter and more level alternative.

START Small parking area for Pwll-y-Wrach nature reserve on a minor road 1 mile SE of Talgarth. There is room for about three cars here. SO 163327. Alternatively park in Talgarth and walk up the lane from the town.

DIRECTIONS From Talgarth, take Bell Street, next to the Bridgend Hotel. Follow this out of the town, past the Black Mountain Business Park. Continue on a narrower lane, soon reaching the Pwll-y-Wrach car park.

1 From the parking area, walk up the road for about 300 yards. Then go through a gate on the right into the Pwll-y-Wrach nature reserve. A narrow footpath runs along the edge of the valley, accompanied by the sound of tumbling water far below. *The river has cut a deep trench here, with trees clinging to the precipitous sides. The cone of Mynydd Troed rises above the woodland on the opposite side of the valley.* The footpath soon follows the line of an old tramway, tracing a route along the edge of the ravine and finishing at the remains of an old quarry which it once served. The path continues on the far side of the quarry. Just after passing through a gap in a fence, turn right down a steep pathway, with stairs to assist. Care may be needed on slippery mud. The main waterfall lies down ahead, through the trees. At the bottom arrive at a viewing platform in front of the waterfall, bearing right through a gate back into the nature reserve, then descending some steep steps with the waterfall on your left.

2 The path continues alongside the river. It will be muddy after wet weather. There is a junction of paths next to an interpretive panel.

To Talgarth
N
START
P

3 At this point there is a short route back, by bearing right along the all ability walkway back to the car park. Otherwise, bear left here and remain on the riverside path, continuing to descend alongside the river. In less than ½ mile keep on the main path as it climbs diagonally away from the river. Soon afterwards, bear right up some steps, leading back to the car park.

All-ability walkway

An all-ability walk way leads directly between points 1 and 3 on the map. To reach this from the car park, don't walk up the lane but take the left hand gate directly from the parking area and follow the upper footpath. The path is suitable for those with limited mobility, pushchairs etc. In ¼ mile reach a junction of paths by an interpretive panel. To reach the waterfall from here, bear left and follow the river upstream on a narrower and rougher path.

Pwll-y-Wrach Nature Reserve

The reserve covers an area of ancient woodland. It is owned and managed by Brecknock Wildlife Trust. Woodland plants include celandine, anemones and bluebells. Bird life includes thrushes, wrens and green woodpeckers. If you are lucky you may spot pied flycatchers, redstarts and long-tailed tits. It may be harder to see nocturnal creatures on a day time walk, but the wood is home to dormice and a variety of bats. For more details about the reserve and to download a leaflet, go to: www.brecknockwildlifetrust. org.uk/pwll-y-wrach.html.

Talgarth

Talgarth straddles the small but energetic rivers, Enig and Ellywe as they drain the ample rainfall of the Black Mountains and head towards the Wye a few miles to the north. The town gained a charter in the early fourteenth century and has always been a lively agricultural centre and market town. The present parish church of St Gwendoline dates from a similar period, though a Celtic monastery on this spot was founded in the fifth century. The scenery around Talgarth epitomises the Borderlands, with dark brooding mountains overlooking fertile valleys and woodlands.

entrance

quarry

2

entrance

Main waterfall

entrance

Pwll-y-Wrach NR

River Enig

3

Lower waterfall

0   Yards   220

Pwll-y-Wrach Lower Waterfall

THE HIGHEST CASTLE IN WALES

DESCRIPTION A short but steep climb leads to Castell Dinas, which commands the top of the Rhiangoll valley, a strategic pass through the mountains between Mid and South Wales. The return route weaves around the back of the castle mounds, through the delightful hollow of Rhyd-y-car.

DISTANCE AND TERRAIN 2½ miles. One steep climb, with good paths, tracks and lanes throughout.

START Dragon's Back car park, next to the Castle Inn, Pengenffordd, about 3½ miles south of Talgarth on the A479 towards Abergavenny. SO 174297. There is a £2 parking charge in an honesty box. Proceeds to charity.

1 From the northern end of the car park, follow the sign to Castell Dinas leading down some steps to a bridleway. Turn right along this lane for 50 yards and then cross a stile on the left. Follow the side of the field to another stile, crossing this and a small stream. A steep ascent then faces you to the top of Castell Dinas. Climb two fields, keeping the fence on your left. A third field, this time with the fence on your right, brings you to the castle site.

2 Reaching the crown of the hill, veer left and weave through a series of mounds, all that now remains of the castle. *There are commanding views from the top. Ahead lies the bulk of the Black Mountains, crowned by the highest peaks of Pen-y-Manllwyn and Waun Fach. To the north the landscape of Mid Wales opens up across the Wye Valley to the hills of Radnorshire and beyond.* At the end of the castle site, the path descends, crossing a defensive ditch and passing an old well, until it reaches the saddle.

3 Ahead the sharp ridge of Y Grib, or Dragon's Back, leads up to the high sum-

mits. *Overhead, there may be a circling buzzard or a floating glider from the nearby flying club.* At the bottom, cross a stile and turn right. Follow the track, through the gap, and then bearing left down the valley, with Y Grib on your left and a wood to the right. After a couple more gates, the path descends more steeply and becomes a hard core track leading down to a hollow in the face of the mountain slope at Rhyd-y-car.

4 At the bottom, turn right, crossing a stream and passing the farmhouse. Continue on the lane for just over ½ mile. At a road junction, turn right and descend to a bridge. Bend sharp left by the riding centre and keep on the lane for another ¼ mile.

5 Where the lane doubles back to the left, keep straight ahead, along a track, soon crossing a ford. Continue along this green lane, gradually ascending for about ½ mile. Just after passing the Castle Inn on the left, find the steps back up to the car park.

Castell Dinas

Originally there was probably an Iron Age fort on this strategic site and some of the ditches are still evident. The location commands the top of the Rhiangoll valley, a key pass between the Usk and Wye valleys. The Normans made use of the position soon after the Conquest and the few masonry remains date from Norman occupation. The castle was sacked twice by Welsh patriots, the first time by Prince Llywelyn ab Iorwerth in 1233 and subsequently by supporters of Owain Glyndŵr in the national uprising in the early fourteenth century. Today it is an atmospheric viewpoint between the pass below and the high mountains above. It is also the highest castle in Wales at nearly 1500 feet above sea level.

The Dragon's Back

From Point 3 the switchback ridge of Y Grib leads to the summit plateau. This is nicknamed the 'Dragon's Back' because of its profile from either side. A full walk up the ridge to Waun Fach, the highest summit in the eastern part of the National Park, is included in Kittiwake's guide to the Black Mountains.

If you want to extend this walk, you could explore the first section of the ridge up to the shelter. However, the full walk is a mountain expedition.

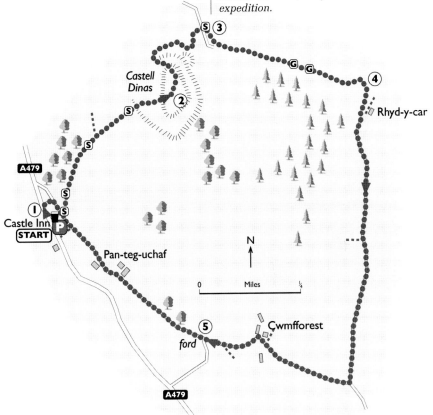

Castell Dinas

WALK 4

A STROLL AROUND LLANGORS LAKE

DESCRIPTION Llangors Lake is the largest natural stretch of water in southern Wales. Access to the lakeshore is generally poor, which is frustrating to walkers but helps to protect the remarkable natural environment and habitat. This walk is the best way of gaining some intimacy with the water's edge and marshes that surround it. Llangors Lake, or Llyn Syfaddan, is not only a wildlife sanctuary. It also has a long historical pedigree, with the remains of an ancient lake settlement overlooked by an Iron Age fort.

DISTANCE AND TERRAIN 3 miles there and back. This is one of the easiest walks in the book; a pleasant stroll on a summer evening. The path follows the shoreline at a discrete distance, offering good opportunities to observe birds and to study the plant life of the marsh. It can be flooded after wet weather.

START Car park, Llangors Common, SO 129273. To reach Llangors, use the B4560 between Talgarth and Bwlch. Follow the signs from Llangors village to the lake. There is a large area of common land and parking is available here. Llangors is not easy to reach by public transport.

I From the car park, cross the access road and take the grass path directly across Llangors Common. Aim for a footbridge at the far side of the common. This crosses the Afon Llynfi. Go through the gate and bear left, following the waymark and crossing the next field diagonally. *The tops of Pen y Fan and Cribyn dominate the western horizon.* Go through the kissing gate at the end of the field and continue in the same direction across the next enclosure, a patch of reeds on the left concealing the lake. Pass through another gate and admire two ancient gnarled oak trees in the next field. Just beyond them, go through a further gate and cross a footbridge over a ditch.

2 At the other side bear left across a water meadow. The path is firm but yellow flag iris and reeds indicate the aqueous terrain on the fringe of the lake. The path takes a slightly elevated position in the next field, offering views across the water back to the jetty and crannog, the remains of an artificial island. *At the top of the field, admire Ty Mawr farmhouse, which appears on maps as early as 1584.* Soon you enter Llangasty Nature Reserve. The reserve is owned by the National Park, and run by the local wildlife trust. A path to the right leads down to a hide on the lakeshore. *If you have time, you can observe the birds and wildlife on the lake.* Continue back on the path above a copse with duckboards now aiding the way in damper places. *Up to your right on the nearest hilltop you can see the remains of Allt yr Esgair, an Iron Age fort dating from 100 CE.* The path traverses a small wood and a series of fields to arrive on a lane in front of Llangasty-Talyllyn church.

3 *Turn right to look at the church, or left to the lakeshore.* There are various paths around the area suggesting a circular return can be made to Llangors Common. In reality, most are difficult to follow, or overgrown. The best idea is to return the way you have come, enjoying views and perspectives in the opposite direction.

Llangors Lake

Covering an area of over 150 hectares, Llangors is the second largest sheet of natural water in Wales, after Llyn Tegid near Bala. It is surrounded by a further 10 hectares of wetland and marsh and fringed by gently shelving shores. Because of these important characteristics, the lake and its surrounds are designated as a site of special scientific interest. On the edge of the water, there are beds of reeds, sedges and rushes. Alder, willow and hazel colonise the water margins. Water lilies can grow in deeper water. Insects and plants thrive here and the lake is a good habitat for dragonflies. It provides an important breeding site for reed warblers and hosts around 20 species of birds during winter including teal, pochard and tufted duck. There are substantial threats to the environ-

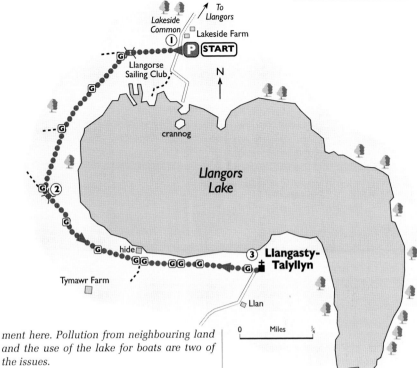

ment here. Pollution from neighbouring land and the use of the lake for boats are two of the issues.

The Crannog

In 1868, the remains of a crannog, or artificial island, were discovered in the lake, near the slipway on the northern shore. This may have been built as a fortified palace and would probably have supported a few buildings. Giraldus Cambriensis (Gerald of Wales), who toured Wales recruiting soldiers for the crusades in the twelfth century, recounted a legend that a city lay beneath the water.

Llangasty-Talyllyn

The church at Llangasty-Talyllyn is the only dedication to St Gastyn in the world. He was probably one of the Celtic Christians who preserved the faith during the inundation of pagan invaders in the fifth and sixth centuries. The existence of a church here dates back many centuries. During the nineteenth century, it was substantially rebuilt as part of the high church Tractarian movement.

Llangors Lake

BRECON, CANAL & RIVER

DESCRIPTION A tour of Brecon and its environs, visiting the upper terminus of the Brecon and Monmouthshire Canal and the few remains of the old railway that linked the waterway with Hay on Wye. Return along the banks of the Usk, exploring the natural environment of Brecon's flood plain.

DISTANCE AND TERRAIN 2½ miles. Almost entirely flat, using roads, tracks and grass paths.

START Main car park by Tourist Information Centre in the centre of Brecon. SO 046285. There are many alternative car parks available, including one near the Marina at point 2.

I Walk through Bethel Square shopping precinct, arriving at the Guild Hall on the High Street. Turn left, walking past the Parish Church, a statue of the Duke of Wellington and the Brecon Museum. Continue ahead into Watton, the main road east. Shortly, turn right into Rich Way, coming to the Marina in a couple of hundred yards.

2 The Marina marks the upper end of the Brecon and Monmouthshire Canal. *The original working waterway reached here in 1800. Today the site has been developed as a tourist destination. It is the terminus for leisure narrowboats and the starting point for shorter cruises along the cut.* Follow the towpath, which is also the beginning of the 58-mile Taff Trail, a cycling and walking route through the Beacons to Cardiff. It is a pleasant promenade alongside the water for about ⅓ mile. A lane crosses the canal at bridge 165. Follow it straight ahead. However, before you completely abandon the towpath, wander along it for another 100 yards to view the interpretation panel on the Hay Railway and Watton Wharf, complete with reconstructed tram and figures. *It outlines how, in 1816, a tramway was opened to connect the waterway with Hay and, later, to Kington.* Return to the lane, which runs

parallel to the canal, and just below it. It follows the course of a branch of the tramway. Pass reconstructed lime kilns built into the canal embankment, and, immediately after these, keep on the lane as it swings right, away from the canal, and towards the sewage works. Continue niftily pass the entrance to this essential utility and head towards the Usk, backed here by the steeply wooded slopes of Coed Nant-y-Ceiliog on the opposite bank.

3 At the end of the track, turn right through a gate and follow the footpath alongside the river through waterside meadows. After a couple of gates, pass through rougher grassland on a terrace above the river, the remains of an old flood plain. *This is now Ministry of Defence property and the path passes the remains of wartime pillboxes.* At a path junction next to a bench, carry straight on, keeping to the river bank. Look across the flood plain to the attractive profile of Brecon, now mercifully bypassed by the A40, whose traffic can be heard across the river. The path follows the river as it curves right and the meadows come to an end by an electricity sub-station. Go through a gate and keep straight ahead on the lane to arrive at a T-junction with the town walls ahead.

4 Turn left and follow the tarmac footpath which returns to the riverside and soon reaches the Usk Bridge. Pass through a gate and climb the steps to the road. If you want to extend the walk you could saunter along Brecon's Promenade. To find this, cross the main road, and follow Watergate, opposite, for a few yards until you reach the beginning of the footpath. Otherwise turn right and follow Ship Street past the library and up into the town. It soon becomes High Street and leads to the Guild Hall, close to the car park and start of the walk.

Brecon

Brecon is a historic and attractive town. It bridges the river Usk at its confluence with the Honddu, on a strategic route to and from western Wales. The Romans built a fort just west of here at Cicucium as a staging post on their road between Gloucester and

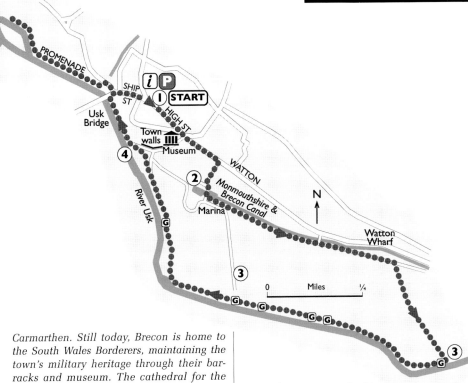

Carmarthen. Still today, Brecon is home to the South Wales Borderers, maintaining the town's military heritage through their barracks and museum. The cathedral for the diocese of Swansea and Brecon is situated on a hill just above the town centre. Originally the church of a Benedictine Priory, it became the town's parish church after the dissolution of the monasteries in the 1530s and was made a cathedral in 1923. A neighbouring sixteenth century tithe barn houses a heritage centre that interprets the history and work of the cathedral. Brecon is an important agricultural centre. Its townscape includes many Georgian buildings as well as some tasteful newer developments, including the terminal basin on the Monmouthshire and Brecon Canal.

Brecon Cathedral

AROUND THE MOUNTAIN CENTRE

DESCRIPTION

Walk 6 explores the heathland north-east of the centre, culminating at the remains of an Iron Age fort overlooking the Usk valley.

Walk 7 heads west, offering extensive views from the old quarry on Allt Lom before crossing Traeth Moor nature reserve and the line of Sarn Helen, the ancient Roman road across Wales.

Distance and terrain Both walks are 3 miles long and offer interesting and gentle excursions around the common land surrounding the National Park Authority's Visitor Centre.

Start Brecon Beacons National Park Mountain Centre, near Libanus, SN 978264. The Mountain Centre is reached by a minor road from the A470 at Libanus, about four miles south of Brecon. It is well signposted.

WALK 6
MYNYDD ILLTUD AND TWYN Y GAER

1 Go through the gate at the far end of the car park to gain access on to the common. Follow the main track ahead north-eastwards and enjoy views right to Pen y Fan and ahead to the Black Mountains. After a while the track passes just above a small marshy pond and soon you come to a minor road. Cross this, carrying straight ahead on the bridleway. *You can now see the trig point crowning Twyn y Gaer ahead.* Another side road is crossed and you take the direct grassy route straight up to the Iron Age fort ahead. Remains of the ditches are still evident and, although the ascent from this side is gentle, once at the top you realise why the fort was established here. In front of you the ground drops steeply away into the Usk valley, a key route to and from western Wales.

2 You can vary your return by following the path just to the left of your ascent.

This curves back round to re-cross the road. Here, follow the bridleway sign towards the Mountain centre. But, after a few yards, instead of continuing on this, veer right to keep on the track next to the wall. Follow the boundary of the common all the way round until you come to a farm access road. (It is also possible to cut across the common directly back to the Mountain Centre at many points.)

3 When you reach the farm access track, turn left along it, cross the road and follow the green track back to the Mountain Centre.

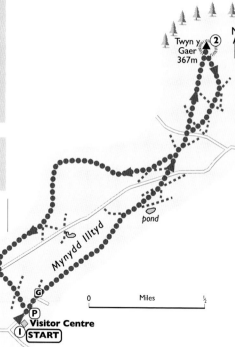

WALK 7
ALLT LOM AND TRAETH MOOR

1 From the centre, walk back along the approach road to its junction with the lane. Turn right (west) and follow the road as it leaves the common over a cattle grid.

Opposite the farm there is an old graveyard in the trees. Its circular shape suggests it may have been a holy site before the arrival of Christianity. The road leaves the enclosure and returns to the common over another cattle grid. At a T-junction, carry straight on. There are a number of tracks. Follow the one next to the wall. After 200 yards, a gate in the wall marks the point where the line of the Roman road, Sarn Helen, crosses the track. There is no obvious trace of this antiquity today. Continue ahead, with the wall on your right. You soon come to a line of beech trees and the craggy remains of an old quarry.

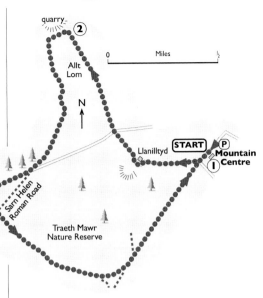

2 An easy, grassy climb to the top is rewarded with excellent views. Carry straight on over the hill. Just beyond the quarry turn left along a green track through the gorse. In 100 yards this meets a rutted track in front of a fence. Turn left along this, with the high peaks of the Beacons now directly ahead. Where the cinder path veers to the left, choose the alternative grassy fork to the right. This accompanies the fence and drops gently down, crossing a farm access lane before joining a minor road. As you near the road, you pick up the line of Sarn Helen again. *The Roman road continued in the direction of a modern pipeline marker, but again there is little in the way of obvious archaeology to evidence this important historic route.* Turn right along the road.

3 Just beyond a couple more pipeline markers and about 100 yards short of a pond, turn sharp left along an earthen track to cross the Traeth Moor nature reserve, an important peat wetland habitat. At the far side of the moor, join another track in front of the boundary fence. Turn left along this back to the Mountain Centre.

The Mountain Centre

The Centre itself is a great focus for a visit. It offers interpretative displays and a video presentation about the national park, as well as a shop, information centre and excellent café. The lawns outside provide a grassy terrace to enjoy spectacular views of the Beacons.

The Visitor Centre

BWLCH & CEFN MOEL

DESCRIPTION A broad, high ridge separates Llangorse and the Rhiangoll valley. Stretching from Mynydd Llangorse to Cefn Moel, this moorland reaches the outskirts of Bwlch. The settlement straddles the lower end of the ridge and this position gives the village its name, meaning a 'pass' or 'col'. This short walk offers an easy excursion on to the airy heathland above Bwlch with extensive views across the Beacons and Black Mountains. The return route uses a quiet cul-de-sac, in season bordered by lush hedgerows and wild flowers.

DISTANCE AND TERRAIN 2 miles, though you can extend the walk along the open high ground of Cefn Moel as far as you like. There is a steep but straightforward climb on to the ridge, followed by easy grass tracks and a quiet lane.

START Bwlch lies on the A40 between Brecon and Abergavenny. The main road makes a right angled turn at the eastern end of the village. The walk starts on this sharp bend, at the junction of the A40 and Tregraig Road. SO 153221. Bwlch is not an easy place to park, but there should be a few places just at the end of Tregraig Road. Some buses between Brecon and Abergavenny pass along the main road.

1 Walk westwards up into the village, using the pavement alongside the A40 for about 300 yards. *There are two bunk houses in Bwlch, the New Inn on the left and, on the right, the white-painted Star Bunk House.* Just in front of the Star, turn right up a gap towards an old chapel. There is a wooden signpost on the wall behind you. Go through the graveyard and pass to the left side of the chapel. Just beyond, find a kissing gate and a footpath leading on uphill.

2 When you reach a lane, turn right and almost immediately, turn left steeply up a track. This soon passes the last house and goes through another gate to gain open hill-side. A very steep ascent follows. The compensation is that you quickly gain height, open heath and wide views. *It's not long before the gradient becomes kinder and you can pause to enjoy a full panorama of the Beacons from flat-capped Pen y Fan (west) to the cone of the Sugar Loaf (east). The wide fields of the Usk Valley are laid out behind you.* The route follows a broad grass track between bracken, brightened by the yellow flash of gorse bushes when in flower. As it continues to ascend, the path comes alongside a fence and wall on the crest of a rising slope. *To the left, there are glimpses down to Llangors Lake, the largest natural sheet of open water in southern Wales. There is evidence of a prehistoric defensive enclosure on the steep slopes to your left.* A small cairn to the right marks the start of the ridge proper. Less than ¼ mile further on, come to a crossing of paths.

3 Ignore the gate on the left, giving access to a bridleway going west. If you feel like it, you can explore the ridge ahead as far as your mood takes you. *There are lovely expansive views, with the limestone bulk of Pen Cerrig Calch rising above the trench of the Rhiangoll valley.* However, the route of this walk turns right at the crossing. Cut along this path for a few yards and very quickly come to a broad track. Turn right here and follow this bridleway for about ¾ mile, gradually descending across open land. It reaches a road near a couple of houses. Go straight across this road and continue along the footpath beyond, passing through a gate and walking downhill on a grassy path. Soon it arrives at the end of a lane next to farm buildings.

4 Turn right here and follow the lane for a mile, back to Bwlch. *In season the hedgerows sport a variety of wild flowers including bluebells, eyebright, celandine, violets, herb Robert, vetch and forget-me-not.*

Bwlch

The village was originally known as Bwlch'r allwys and is surrounded by a range of historical locations. The A40 is only a successor to a far older route. The Romans built a road between Abergavenny and Brecon, cutting through the pass at Bwlch and continuing westwards over the slopes of Allt yr Esgair. Two miles to the east of Bwlch they built an auxiliary fort at Pen-y-gaer. A little further east lies the Norman castle at Tretower and the adjacent fortified manor house at Tretower Court, now cared for by Cadw.

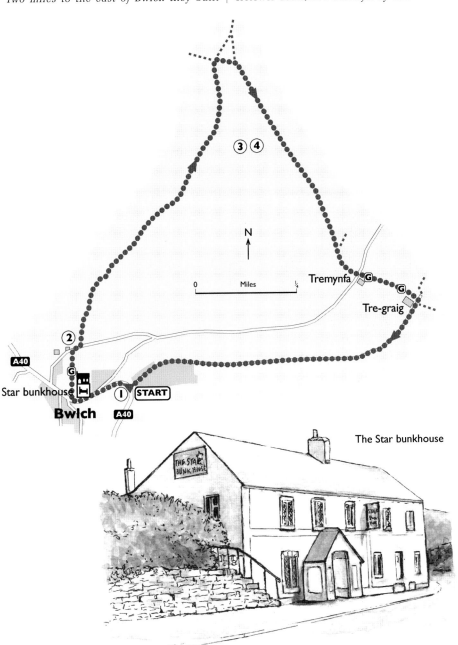

The Star bunkhouse

COED-Y-CERRIG
&
FOREST COALPIT

DESCRIPTION An easy circuit around the charming Coed-y-Cerrig Nature Reserve and the surrounding countryside in the Grwyne Fawr valley. Explore ancient woodland, valley pastures and wetlands.

DISTANCE AND TERRAIN 2 miles. Woodland paths, quiet lanes and tracks, with some short climbs. The final section follows a duckboard trail through wetland. There are shorter options within the reserve itself.

START There is a small car park for the Nature Reserve, on the north side of the road between Llanfihangel Crucorney and Forest Coal Pit, SO 294212.

DIRECTIONS To reach Coed-y-Cerrig, leave the A465 at Llanfihangel Crucorney and follow the road towards Llanthony. In just over a mile, take the left turn towards Forest Coal Pit. After another 1¼ miles, watch out carefully for the car park on the right hand side of the road.

1 There are two footpaths out of the small car park. Take the right hand option and climb steeply up the woodland bank. In season, bluebells, violets, and herb Robert carpet the floor of the reserve. The path curves round to the left and then arrives at a stile leading out of the wood. Continue ahead into a magical, hidden meadow, framed by trees, aiming for the left hand side of the old house at the far end of the meadow. *This is known as The Pant.* Pass a pond on the way. At the end, a stile at the left hand corner of the meadow takes the footpath around the boundary of the houses and onto a track beyond. *The gardens, blossom trees and hedges around the buildings are magnificent.* The track leads onto a driveway, and reaches a lane.

2 At the end of the driveway, turn left and walk down the lane to the crossroads at the bottom. *This is the valley of the Grwyne Fawr, draining the high ridges of the Black Mountains and feeding the waters of the Usk. The great profile of the Sugar Loaf dominates the view ahead.* At the crossroads, keep straight ahead onto the minor road beyond. Follow this for about 200 yards before turning left over a stile to follow a footpath across a field. A fingerpost confirms the route and the direction to walk across the field. At the far side, another stile leads to a small footbridge over a ditch. A further stile leads to a short climb and a gravelled path through mixed woodland and holly trees. Climb across a final field to reach the road; you need to negotiate a sturdy but rather awkward stone stile!

3 Turn left and follow the lane. Pass the old chapel and graveyard on the right. *There is evidence of prehistoric settlement all around this area. Up to the right, crowning the flattish topped hill, is the Iron Age camp at the Gaer. Turning round and looking back the way you've come, notice the flat top of Crug Hywel, another Iron Age camp just above Crickhowell.* Continue past Chapel Farm until the lane ends at Forest Coal Pit Farm. Here keep straight ahead, going through a gate on to the track beyond. 200 yards after the gate, the track splits. Turn left, leaving the main track to continue towards Stanton. Instead, turn left here and descend a walled green lane, dropping diagonally down the wooded hillside back in to Coed-y-Cerrig.

4 As you reach the valley floor, watch out for a junction with a boardwalk. Turn left here, taking the wooden causeway across the wetland and passing an information board telling you more about the reserve. *Alder and willow thrive in this habitat. Further up, ash hazel and birch cling to the steep banks of this side valley of the Grwyne Fawr, while beech and oak crown the top. The wet floor hosts early purple orchids, bluebells, bellflowers and marsh marigolds.* Where the path splits you can stay on the boardwalk or opt for the wood mulch path. Both will bring you back to the road opposite the car park and this section is suitable for all abilities.

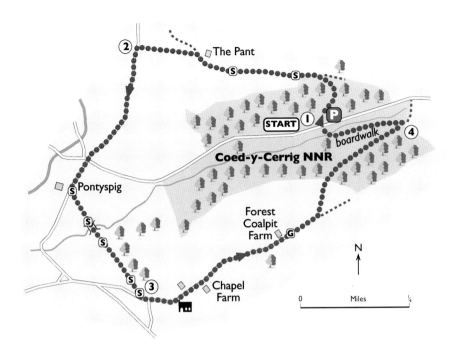

Coed-y-Cerrig National Nature Reserve

Tucked into a sheltered wooded valley hidden in the heart of the Black Mountains, Coed-y-Cerrig is a small but important national nature reserve, managed by the Countryside Council for Wales. The reserve is divided by a minor road, paved over an old railway. The line was built to serve the construction of the Grwyne Fawr reservoir dam on the edge of the high moors to the north. The valley's fast flowing stream is itself a tributary of the Grwyne Fawr. Coed-y-Cerrig
means 'wood of stones' and this is an apt description for its secluded enchantment. The first part of the walk climbs hillside woodland, with beech and oak among the rocky outcrops. The floor of the reserve (from Point 4) is silted wetland, a rare example of alluvial forest. Here alder and willow flourish and a boardwalk provides access through the intimate heart of the wetland. The floor of the reserve is carpeted by an extensive array of wild flowers including wood anemones, primroses and foxgloves.

Grwyne Fawr valley

MYNYDD DDU

DESCRIPTION The forest of Mynydd Ddu cloaks the upper reaches of the Grwyne Fawr valley, scything deep into the heart of the Black Mountains. A single cul-de-sac road leads up to the head of the valley, giving access to the core of the hills. With its relative isolation, there are many opportunities to observe the flowers, trees and wildlife of the forest and mountainside. In spring you will hear, and if lucky see, pairs of breeding cuckoos. Wild ponies graze on the open mountainside, while woodpeckers fly across the trees. An initial climb into the forest leads to a promenade around the mountain, offering a magnificent panorama of the highest peaks of the Black Mountains.

DISTANCE AND TERRAIN 4 miles. The route follows forest tracks and mountain paths. There is one significant climb at the beginning and a steady descent later.

START Forestry car park at Pont Cadwgan, which is accessed by a bridge across the river from the valley road. SO 267252. The valley road is a cul-de-sac, which starts at the crossroads at Forest Coal Pit. It follows the Grwyne Fawr River northwards into the Black Mountains. Forest Coalpit can be accessed by narrow lanes from Crickhowell or by leaving the A465 at Llanfihangel Crucorney, four miles north of Abergavenny.

I With the bridge behind you, take the left hand track. This crosses a small stream and climbs steadily up the small side valley of Nant-y-Gwerydd in company with the stream tumbling downhill on the right. Soon, beech and sycamore trees give way to conifers. Keep climbing for about ½ mile, ignoring any side turnings. At the top, the track turns sharply to the left. Instead of doubling back on this track, continue ahead, very soon reaching a broad forest road. Turn left to follow it.

2 The forest road contours the side of the hill – *with great views now across the forests of Mynydd Ddu and the Grwyne Fawr valley. Looking back, you can see the distinctive profile of the Skirrid.* Emerge from

woodland into an area of felled trees and, soon afterwards, leave the forest altogether. About ½ mile along the forest road, watch out for a stile crossing into the first open field on the right. If you're going downhill on the forest road, you've missed it and will need to retrace your steps to look. Turn right across the stile, climb up the side of the field. About halfway up, watch out for a marker post to the left. This indicates the direction of another stile, which in turn gives access to the open hillside. Cross this and continue uphill on the public footpath for about 200 yards, where a broad path crosses. *The dome of Bal Mawr lies ahead. Although its skyline is not particularly notable or dramatic, it is the highest point in Monmouthshire at 607metres.*

3 Turn right and follow the path on a level course around the hillside. It keeps company intermittently with edge of the forest below, while on the upper side of the route, bilberries, heather and bracken cover the hillside. After about a mile, the terrain opens out. For a while the path remains level, the cone of the Sugar Loaf in the distance. Later, it gradually descends to the narrowing ridge just below some walled enclosures. *From here you can see the ridge ahead is quite slender and the valleys either side are not far apart, but they drain in completely different directions. To the right, the Grwyne Fawr feeds the Usk and flows south to Newport. To the left the Honddu feeds the Monnow which in turn leads to a confluence with the Wye at Monmouth.* Continue along the crest of the ridge, arriving at a stone set by the side of the path, near a wall corner.

4 Turn sharp right here, not following the wall itself, but taking a broad grass track going downhill. This shortly crosses another track and continues descending the hillside diagonally and heading back into the valley of the Grwyne Fawr. The path drops more steeply through gorse bushes and then joins a wall between the forest and the open hillside. Go through a gate and continue along the green lane beyond. Pass a house and follow the access road to the bottom, crossing a bridge onto the valley road.

5 Turn right along the road. You can simply follow the road for about a mile back to the start. It's quiet and wide enough to avoid close encounters with any traffic there is. If you don't like road walking, bear left in 100 yards to follow a footpath sign. You climb back into the woods to join a forest road. Turn right and descend back to the car park.

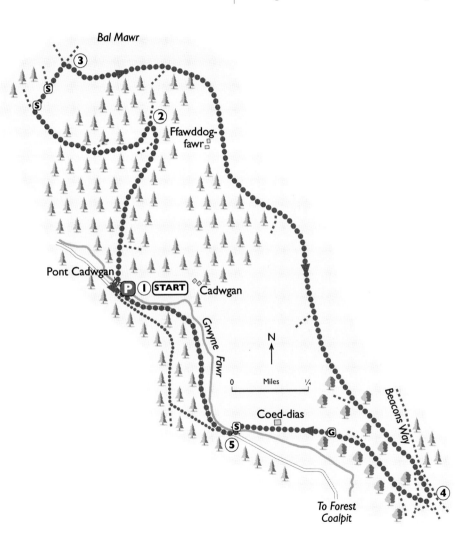

THE SUGAR LOAF

DESCRIPTION The Sugar Loaf's distinctive profile is recognisable from as far east as the Cotswold escarpment. It marks the point where the Usk emerges from the wilder uplands of the Brecon Beacons into the lush and fertile pastures of Monmouthshire. This is an interesting circuit of the mountain from the south, starting at a high level and so reducing the amount of climbing. Even so this is real upland country and do not underestimate the challenge! The rewards are fantastic views with an airy sense of space and freedom.

DISTANCE AND TERRAIN 3 miles. Paths and tracks across open mountainside with a steep climb to the summit. Landscape is exposed so have warm clothing, waterproofs and boots. There are lots of paths and tracks on the Sugar Loaf, which makes it great for exploring in good weather. But the plethora of routes can also make it confusing, especially in mist. In poor visibility take and use a compass, especially on the summit.

START Car Park on Llanwenarth Common. SO 267167. A narrow lane leaves the A40 on the western outskirts of Abergavenny. Signs to Sugar Loaf Vineyard point you in the right direction. Pass the vineyard to continue climbing up the slopes of the Sugar Loaf. After a while the lane turns west and climbs around the side of the mountain to reach a good car park. This is an excellent viewpoint over the Usk valley and the Brecon Beacons. It also offers a bird's eye view of Abergavenny.

1 From the car park by the old toposcope walk back down the road towards Abergavenny for about ¼ mile. There is a rough parking area on the left hand side from where a broad, grassy path leaves the road, bearing left across the open hillside. Take this path for about ¼ mile, ignoring any side turnings. It approaches a wood and curves to the left, contouring round the side of the hill. It enters the wood and descends slightly to join another path coming in from the right.

2 Bear left here to join this path which continues above the edge of a wooded valley intruding into the great bulk of the Sugar Loaf, St Mary's Vale. The trees gradually thin and the route now climbs along the side of St Mary's Vale, with the summit of the mountain now looming ahead. As you approach the head of the valley, look out for a solitary tree with a path bearing right and heading directly for the summit. Although paths are narrower now, they are generally clear. The route rounds the head of the valley, here called Cwm Trosnant. Keep forward, following the path up a small groove. Continue up until you meet a cross track.

3 At this point, keep straight ahead, to follow a broader path, and aiming resolutely for the summit of the Sugar Loaf. The last section is steep and as the top approaches there are more rocks and crags. The compact summit is actually a short east-west ridge, with the trig point at the western end.

4 From the top, take a path branching off the western end of the ridge and descending the mountainside diagonally in a WSW direction. Make sure you don't stay on the ridge on the other broad path heading WNW. You quickly lose height and the track becomes a very broad grassy swathe with great views across the Usk Valley to the Blorenge on the other side.

5 When the path becomes more level, come to a crossing with another grassy track. Turn right here; it soon veers back round to the left, above the wooded valley of Cwm Gwenffrwd. It continues to descend and leads around the side of the hill back to the car park.

The Sugar Loaf

There are 'three peaks' surrounding Abergavenny, the Skirrid (Ysgyryd Fawr), the Blorenge (Blorens) and the Sugar Loaf (Y Fal). All are distinctive but the conical profile of the Sugar Loaf explains its obvious English name. The summit falls just short of 2000 feet (1955). The land is owned and managed by the National Trust and is founded on sandstone, with quartz outcrops at the highest levels of the mountain. The cone is encircled by deciduous woodland, while the upper slopes host heather and bilberry. The Sugar Loaf is the only Welsh mountain to sport a vineyard, situated off the approach road at the foot of the mountain.

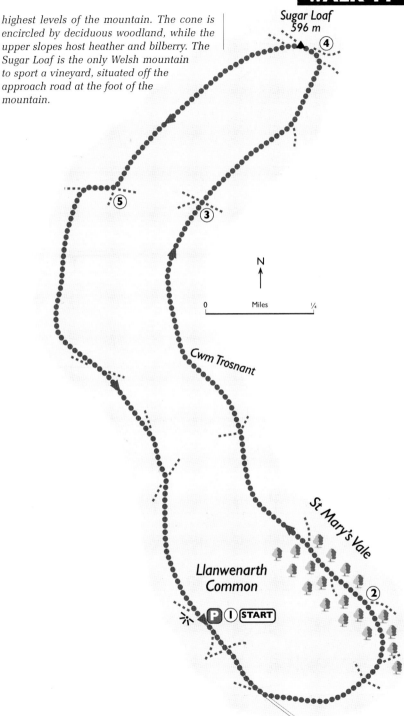

Sugar Loaf
596 m

④

⑤

③

N

0   Miles   ¼

Cwm Trosnant

St Mary's Vale

②

Llanwenarth
Common

P ⓘ START

THE TRAMWAY, THE PUNCHBOWL & THE CUT

DESCRIPTION The tranquillity of this rural hillside conceals a vibrant industrial past. The wharf at Llanfoist was an interchange for the transportation of iron and coal from Blaenavon to the busy docks at Newport. The first part of the walk climbs the steep incline that brought the coal and iron down to the canal. A well-graded path then contours the mountain to reach the secluded Punchbowl nature reserve. The return route uses the canal towpath, a peaceful and level walk with an occasional pleasure boat lingering along the cut.

DISTANCE AND TERRAIN 5 miles. A steep ascent up the line of an old tramway incline, followed by an undulating contoured route on paths and lanes around the wooded slopes of the Blorenge. Return route is along canal towpath.

START Llanfoist Crossing car park. SO 286134. Llanfoist village lies on the B4246 just a mile south of Abergavenny. Reach it from the intersection with the A465 Heads of the Valleys dual carriageway, ½ mile from the roundabout with the A40 and A4042.

I Llanfoist Crossing car park is on the north side of the road, on the line of the old railway track from Brynmawr. This is now a cycleway. Go out of the car park and cross the main road. Continue up the lane opposite, signposted to the Blorenge, with the church on your left. At the top of the lane, continue straight ahead, climbing through a tunnel under the canal. This brings you to Llanfoist wharf. *Thomas Hill built a tram road through the Blorenge to carry iron and coal from Blaenavon. This saved the expensive tolls and challenging terrain of the direct route to Newport, down the Eastern Valley through Abersychan. The tram road tunnelled through the Blorenge then contoured*

round the side of the hill. It ended at a winch where a series of three inclines lowered cargo to the wharf on the canal at Llanfoist. A couple of replica trams remind you of this history. The incline was worked by gravity. Loaded trucks going downhill pulled the empty ones back up the slope. The path takes this incline on the far side of the canal, following an unremittingly steep climb through the woods and beside a stream. *Many of the stone sleepers that held the two-foot gauge track in place can still be seen. The top of the first part of the incline is marked by an old brick building, which houses a cistern for a nearby farm.* Keep straight ahead and climb on up the hill, crossing some side tracks and a number of stiles. Eventually come to the boundary of open land.

2 Cross a stile over the fence and come onto the open mountainside. Pause to admire the view behind. *The distinctive profiles of the Skirrid and the Sugar Loaf rise beyond the townscape of Abergavenny. Together with the Blorenge, these three hills are sometimes referred to as the 'three peaks' of Abergavenny.* Turn left immediately after the fence and follow a lovely path, contouring round the edge of the Blorenge just above the intake wall. After a while a gate gives access to a Woodland Trust nature reserve. Continue through the reserve on a good path. *The faint buzz of noise from the valley is drowned by birdsong. Green woodpeckers, buzzards and tawny owls can be seen here and a variety of woodland birds fly from the range of trees scattered across the hillside.* The path comes to a small lake in a glacial hollow known as the Punchbowl. Turn left across the dam wall. The path continues up the side of the hollow, next to a fence and among beech trees, weaving up to a gate.

3 Go through the gate and turn left and downhill on to a wide green lane, which soon becomes a sunken track. It meanders back to the left and comes to a road. Turn right here and climb the lane.

4 In about ¼ mile, by a road junction and a small pull-in area, turn left and cross a stile. The route is signposted to Llanellen.

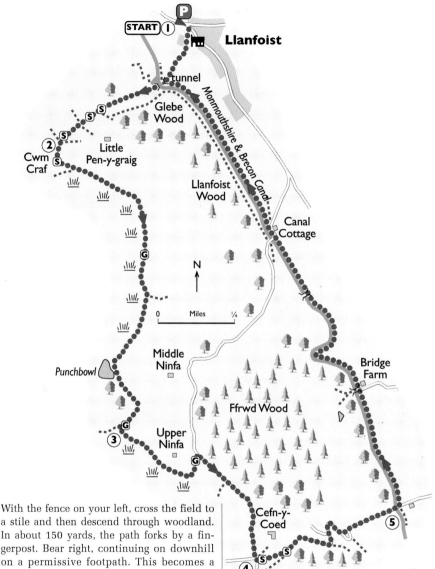

With the fence on your left, cross the field to a stile and then descend through woodland. In about 150 yards, the path forks by a fingerpost. Bear right, continuing on downhill on a permissive footpath. This becomes a stony, sunken lane. Where this stony path ends, bend sharp left, keeping on the main track, rather than going in the direction of the fingerpost, through a conifer wood. Descend with the fence on your right, soon coming to a road end by a couple of houses. Continue on the lane, which winds down the hill. When it crosses the canal, go through the gate onto the towpath.

5 Continue along the towpath back towards Llanfoist for about 1½ miles. When you arrive at Llanfoist Wharf, climb down the steps to the right to join the lane back to the start.

23

WALK 13

TAF FECHAN FOREST

DESCRIPTION A tour around the headwaters of the Taf Fechan, visiting forest clearings and a disused reservoir. The walk penetrates the heart of the Beacons without climbing their steep slopes!

DISTANCE AND TERRAIN 4 miles. Excellent tracks and paths for most of the route and only one stile.

START Car park at Pont Cwmyfedwen, SO 043164. To reach here, take the minor road that crosses the Beacons between Talybont-on-Usk and Merthyr. This is a spectacular traverse in itself, linking the Taf Fechan and Caerfanell valleys to carve a route through the remote spine of the mountain massif. Although it is a high-level mountain route, it is a good road. A cul de sac leads north off it at a sharp bend, close to the head of Pentwyn reservoir. Follow this for about ½ mile. Just after it crosses the Taf Fechan at Pont Cwmyfedwen, find the car park on the right.

1 From the car park, turn left and walk back along the road. Cross the bridge and about 300 yards beyond it, take the first forest road which leaves the road sharply to the right. Pass a barrier and walk ahead along a level course, the forest road soon giving way to a good track. *There are tantalising glimpses of the higher summits of the Beacons as the track gently rises and passes through clearings in the forest. Oak trees and other natural species now liberate the woodland from the dreary awning of dark conifers.* Later the track becomes a path but the way remains clear and there is only one significantly boggy patch. Over a mile after leaving the road cross a stile next to a small standing stone and then climb up to a gate on to the Lower Neuadd dam.

2 *Lower Neuadd Reservoir was opened in 1884 to quench the thirst of Merthyr's industrial workforce. It is now a drained hollow, surrounded by a broken hiatus of former*

workings. Turn right to walk across the dam, then dip down and up past the old filter house to reach a gate and cattle grid, leading to a track. Turn left. In 100 yards come to a T-junction with another track and turn left again. In a further 200 yards, turn right through a gate and climb up a stony track. In 300 yards, arrive at a T junction.

3 The main track turns left here. *This is an ancient route towards Brecon that crosses the ridge of the Beacons at 'The Gap'.* Leave that for another day and for now, turn right, pausing for a moment to enjoy the views across the remains of the reservoir and over to the main peaks of the Beacons. The stony path makes a short but sharp dip to cross a gulley carrying a small stream. On the opposite side, pass through a gate and continue along a good stony track on the far side. In about ½ mile, this sidles up to the tarmac road coming directly from the Lower Neuadd. You touch the road but then immediately leave it to bear left, talking the Taff Trail along a level fenced track. *There are lovely views across the valley to your right, with the open field rolling down to the road and forest beyond. Ahead, the graceful shape of Pentwyn reservoir fills the floor of the valley.* This pleasant, contouring terrace continues for about ¾ mile, before it reaches a gate and joins another forest track. This curves round the hillside, amidst the trees, for just under ½ mile until it comes to the Merthyr-Talybont road, close to its highest point at Torpantau. There is a junction of paths just short of the road. *Nearby is the present terminal point of the Brecon Mountain Railway, which has climbed from Pontsticill on the outskirts of Merthyr.*

4 Turn sharp right, almost doubling back, and follow the forest road downhill. This is Cycleway 8 which traverses Wales from Holyhead to Chepstow. Continue for about ½ mile to return to the car park and start point.

Brecon Mountain Railway
The present Brecon Mountain Railway line extends from Pant, on the outskirts of Merthyr, to Torpantau, close to Point 4 on this walk. It runs along the track bed of the

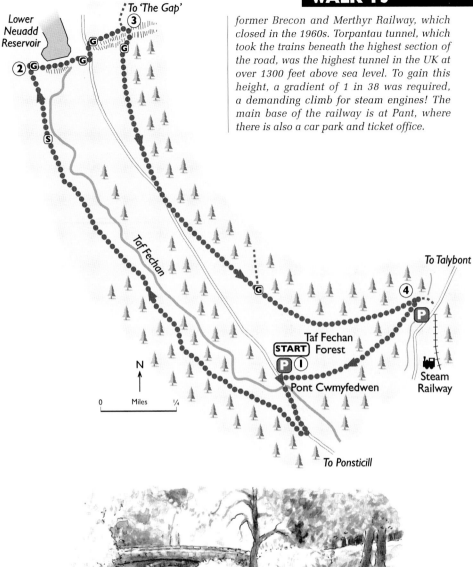

former Brecon and Merthyr Railway, which closed in the 1960s. Torpantau tunnel, which took the trains beneath the highest section of the road, was the highest tunnel in the UK at over 1300 feet above sea level. To gain this height, a gradient of 1 in 38 was required, a demanding climb for steam engines! The main base of the railway is at Pant, where there is also a car park and ticket office.

Pont Cwmyfedwen

CWMTAF FOREST & LLWYN-ON RESERVOIR

DESCRIPTION An easy tour of Cwmtaf Forest, using woodland tracks with easy gradients. The visitor centre at Garwnant offers a café, information and toilets. There is also a children's playground and a series of waymarked paths and cycle routes. This walk follows a modified version of one of the cycle routes. Small brown markers indicate the cycle route. Multi-use paths always require care, but the track is quiet and you are generally unlikely to encounter more than an occasional dog walker (and dog).

DISTANCE AND TERRAIN 4½ miles. Waymarked tracks and paths. Except for the last avoidable short cut path, the whole route is accessible for wheelchairs and pushchairs. The return leg includes a section along the access road from Llwyn-on dam.

START Garwnant Forest Visitor Centre, SO 003131. Garwnant is the centre for Cwmtaf woodlands. An approach road leads from the A470 Merthyr – Brecon road, five miles north of Merthyr. Parking is available at the centre (fee payable).

I From the parking area, walk back down the approach road for a few yards. Where it bends to the left by a couple of disabled parking spaces, turn right and follow the cycle and footpath waymarks along a forest road. Pass the barrier and almost immediately bear left to follow the footpath instead of the track. *There is a stream just down to the left and some duckboards offer the opportunity to explore a pond and marshy area.* The footpath soon crosses a bridge and then turns left at a blue way mark. Climb gently up through the woods to meet a forest track.

2 Turn left and follow this track as it descends gently through the forest. *After a while the trees thin out and there are good views over Llwyn-on reservoir.* After a right

hand bend the track climbs gradually. Ignore a left hand branch and continue following occasional brown cycle track signs. The track curves to the right and then comes to a junction. Turn sharp left here (waymark). The gradual ascent continues. After another 400 yards or so, turn left at a slate sign and way mark.

3 Cross a minor road at Pen-yr-heol and continue with the track on the opposite side. A little later the track bends left and you soon come to a junction. Turn left, following the signs. Now the path continues to descend and the views open out over the reservoir and back over the highest Beacons. Eventually it reaches the reservoir access road.

4 Turn left to follow this road, also part of the Taff Trail, a long distance walking and cycling route from Cardiff to Brecon. It is a quiet access lane, but there is still some traffic, especially on summer weekends or during holiday periods, so take care. Unfortunately access to the shoreline is restricted to permit holders with fishing rods. Nevertheless, the views across the water are picturesque.

5 As you approach the head of the reservoir, immediately after crossing a stream, there is a green post marked with 'H9' and decorated with red and white tape. TURN LEFT up a footpath here. This leads back through the woods a short distance to the car park and visitor centre.

Llwyn-on reservoir

Llwyn-on reservoir was built by Cardiff Corporation and opened in 1926. It is one of three reservoirs in this valley serving Wales' capital city and has a capacity of 5.5 million litres. A plaque on the left also helpfully reminds you that the average rainfall here is 67 inches a year.

Taff Trail

The Taff Trail is a long distance walking and cycling route between Cardiff and Brecon.

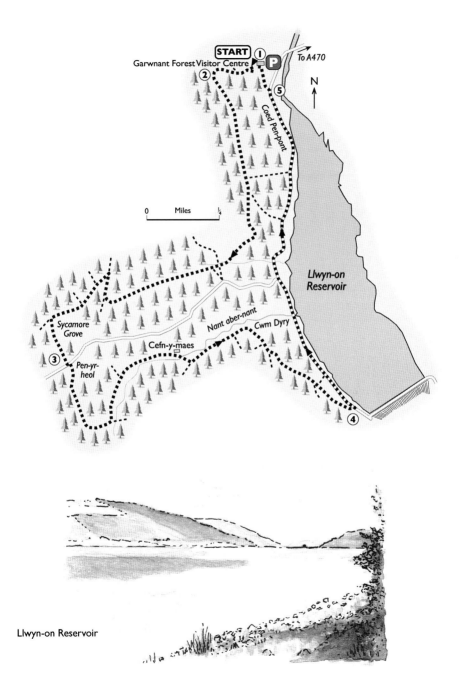

Llwyn-on Reservoir

THE ELIDIR TRAIL

DESCRIPTION The Mellte, Hepste and Nedd Fechan all drain the wild limestone uplands in the southern part of the national park. As they travel south, they cross belts of harder sandstone rock, which the water has eroded less than the neighbouring shale. Here is where the waterfalls are formed and it is a popular area of the national park, often referred to as 'Waterfall Country'. There is a range of walks for all abilities. Paths pass through wooded gorges where fast flowing streams tumble down spectacular waterfalls on their way from the mountains to the sea.

This linear walk is known as the 'Elidir Trail' and follows the fast flowing Nedd Fechan up a series of falls between Pontneddfechan and Pont Melin Fach. This is a simple out-and-back walk along a dramatic and picturesque valley.

DISTANCE AND TERRAIN 5 miles there and back. For the first mile, a good level path, suitable for all abilities. Beyond the footbridge, the path is rougher with some rocky sections and tree roots. It is not particularly difficult, but it is slippery in places and good footwear is needed.

START Opposite the Angel Hotel, Pontneddfechan. SN 902076. There are toilets, a small car park and some roadside parking here. The village of Pontneddfechan lies close to the A465 Hirwaun-Neath road. Leave this main road at Glyn-neath and follow the signs.

I Pass through the iron gates marked 'Sgwd Gwladus'. Follow the path, which is suitable for pushchairs and wheelchairs for the first mile. A deep gorge has been cut through sandstone and some huge overhanging cliffs, Farewell Rock, lie above the left hand side of the path. It follows the line of an old tramway and the stone setts are still visible in places. *The tracks were used by horse drawn trams which carried silica to the Neath Canal nearby.* Mixed deciduous woodland, including sycamore, beech and oak trees, provide habitats for a variety of woodland birds. You may see grey wagtails or dippers in the river itself. Ferns, lichen and violets adorn the surroundings. A picnic area marks the end of the tramway and the limit of navigation for pushchairs and wheelchairs. Beyond are the remains of an old corn mill and nearby is the entrance to the silica mine. The path continues up some steps and onwards to the confluence of the Nedd Fechan and Pyrddin at Pwll Du ar Byrddin.

2 There is a footbridge here, but it's worth branching off to visit Sgwd Gwladus (the 'Lady Fall') first. To do so, continue on the left hand bank. The riverside path continues for about 300 yards, passing a small fall and then ending at a viewing platform just before the cascade at Sgwd Gwladus. Return along the path to the footbridge at Point 2. Cross the footbridge and keep to the left hand side of the Nedd Fechan. The path clings to the side of the river, passing a series of waterfalls. Ravines cut into the cliffs, gouged out by water cascading down into the river below. At first, the path climbs up to overlook the gorge, now moving into limestone, characteristic of the Waterfall country. In a while, pass a series of rapids and waterfalls, culminating in Sgwd Ddwili Uchaf (the upper gushing torrent), where the Nedd Fechan tumbles over a rock ledge into a rock pool below. The final section is more tranquil, but some more falls herald the approach of the picnic area at Pont Melin Fach.

3 The gorge opens out at the picnic area at Pont Melin Fach. There is a car park here and the walk could equally be started here. Return by outward route.

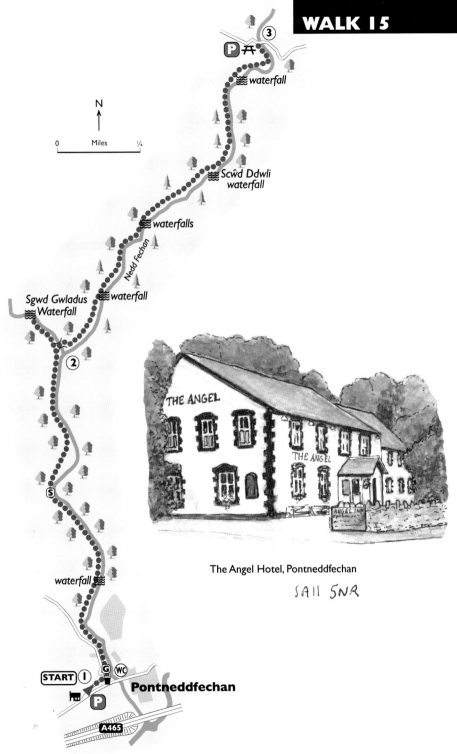

N

0   Miles   ¼

③

waterfall

Scwd Ddwli
waterfall

waterfalls

Nedd Fechan

waterfall

Sgwd Gwladus
Waterfall

②

S

waterfall

The Angel Hotel, Pontneddfechan

SA11 5NR

waterfall

START   **I**   **G**   **WC**

P

Pontneddfechan

A465

29

SARN HELEN & LIMESTONE COUNTRY

DESCRIPTION An exhilarating exploration of the wild uplands around the head of the Nedd Fechan. The route crosses limestone pastures, broken by rocky crags and dotted with limekilns. Part of the route follows the line of Sarn Helen, the Roman road from Neath to Brecon. There is real variety of scenery and, above all, a sense of space and freedom.

DISTANCE AND TERRAIN 5 miles, on tracks and paths with no sustained hills. Although not a mountain walk, much of the route is through wild and desolate country, so go prepared with suitable clothing.

START Ystradfellte village car park, SN 930134. Ystradfellte is accessed by a minor road, which crosses the mountains between Pontneddfechan and Sennybridge.

1 Take the narrow lane up the hill by the side of the car park. Where the tarmac ends, carry straight on up a sunken green lane. At the top a gate leads into open country. The track keeps ascending gently though limestone pasture, dotted with rocks and occasional hawthorn trees. Higher up another gate carries the track into an area of shattered limestone crags. You pass a few ponds and, on your right, a restored lime kiln, offering evidence of the industrial importance of this area in times past. Just past the kiln, cross a stile and join a green lane. Ahead, the rounded tops of Fan Nedd and Fan Llia rise above the wild moors and forest. In about ¾ mile the lane comes to a road, the mountain pass over to Sennybridge. Follow the road left and ascend gently through moors and trees. You pass a Forestry Commission car park on the right at Blaen Llia.

2 A few hundred yards further, turn sharp left through a gate on to a stony track, signposted 'Sarn Helen', a cross-mountain Roman road between forts near Brecon and at Neath. You have now also joined the route of the Beacons Way. Soon pass through the site of a Roman Camp. *This is an atmospheric traverse of wild and lonely country, all the more so on a grey or misty day, when you can imagine the legions of soldiers or solitary farmers crossing these uplands.* Just after a second gate, pass an isolated standing stone, Maen Madoc. Continue through remote upland country, now dropping to the Nedd Fechan. Cross the river using a new wooden footbridge that replaces the risky ford. Follow the track up the opposite bank with the buildings of Blaen Nedd Fechan below you to the left. At the top of the hill, go through a gate to a junction of paths. Leave the Beacons Way here, instead turning left to stay on Sarn Helen. The Beacons Way crosses desolate limestone moor to reach Penwyllt, about 4 miles distant above the upper Swansea valley. Our route and the line of the Roman road coincide beside a wood to another gate. In another 50 yards, come to a junction of paths.

3 At the junction, turn left on to another track. *This is a delightful descent through hawthorn trees to the river.* Cross the bridge and continue up the other side to meet the road. Turn left. In about 200 yards, turn right through a gate, following the bridleway sign to Ystradfellte. Cross a small field and then continue up through a patch of young rowan trees. A gate at the top leads to open heath. Cross this limestone country through series of gates. Just over the brow of the hill, go through a final gate to a big expanse of open land. There is no obvious route on the ground from here, but the bridleway just crosses the rough pasture in the direction indicated by the marker. Cross a track in a depression in the middle of the rough ground. Continue on to reach a gate in the far corner of the enclosure. Go through this to re-join the outward route. Follow the track back down to Ystradfellte.

Sarn Helen

Sarn Helen refers to a Roman road that weaved across Wales from Caernarfon to Conwy, around 160 miles. There is not unanimous agreement about its precise course or

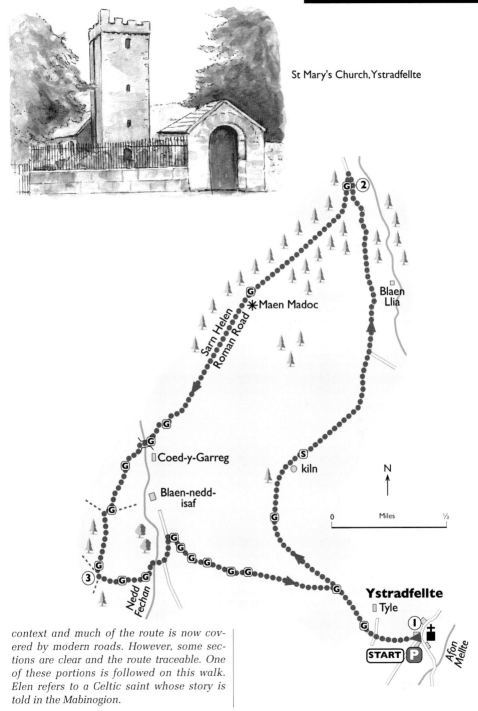

St Mary's Church, Ystradfellte

Maen Madoc

Sarn Helen
Roman Road

Blaen
Llia

Coed-y-Garreg

kiln

Blaen-nedd-
isaf

N

0   Miles   ½

Nedd
Fechan

Ystradfellte
Tyle

START

context and much of the route is now covered by modern roads. However, some sections are clear and the route traceable. One of these portions is followed on this walk. Elen refers to a Celtic saint whose story is told in the Mabinogion.

EXPLORING OGOF FFYNNON DDU

DESCRIPTION Ogof Ffynnon Ddu, 'cave of the black spring', is a National Nature Reserve on the flanks of the upper Swansea Valley and over 1000 feet above sea level. The reserve is a mixture of moorland and limestone pavement overlaying the millstone grit and limestone on the southern edge of the national park. Far beneath the ground, an extensive cave system burrows through the bedrock. Around the periphery, industrial remains add interest to the scene. Paths are limited but this walk makes use of old trails and track-beds to explore the dramatic upland scenery.

DISTANCE AND TERRAIN 2 miles. Moorland exploration with tracks, paths and some old industrial sites

START Car parking area by Penwyllt Quarry. SN 855157. Penwyllt is about a mile from the A4067 Swansea-Brecon road. Take the minor road leaving the main road between Ynyswen and Glyntawe which climbs up to Penwyllt.

1 Walk along the track towards the buildings, which form the base for the South Wales Caving Club. Just in front of the houses, turn left to take a track signposted, 'Entrance to the nature reserve'. Follow the track and soon come to another gate marking the boundary of the Ogof Ffynnon Ddu Nature Reserve. Beyond the gate the track weaves around to meet an embankment, the course of an old tramway.

2 Bear left here and walk uphill on the track bed heading for a cutting in the rocks at the top. *There are rail remnants here and there, including old wooden sleepers.*

3 Just after the cutting, watch out for a grass track on the right. *(If you want to explore the main track further, keep straight ahead here and pass through a further gate. A wide vista of the upper Swansea valley*

opens up. Later, the track curves to the right, passing above the valley of Nant Byfre. After a mile it joins a hard core track. Explore at will and just turn back when you're ready!) To stay on the circular walk, turn right after the cutting, onto the grass track. Continue over the brow and then pass a pothole entrance on the left. The track joins up with the Beacons Way, by a marker post. Turn left and walk along the Beacons Way track to explore the limestone pavement area on the left. *(You can also continue beyond this if you want to explore further).*

4 At the appropriate moment, turn round and retrace your steps, continuing downhill as far as the tramway crossing at Point 2. Here turn left and follow the course of the tramway above the South Wales Caving Club buildings. Continue through some old industrial remains, just above the old railway track. Cross a bridge over this track and go through a gate on the far side.

5 Immediately afterwards turn right. Follow the fence to another gate, which gives access onto the track bed itself. Follow this until another gate leads back to the car park and the starting point.

Ogof Ffynnon Ddu

Hidden below ground at Ogof Ffynnon Ddu is a 30 mile network of caverns, passages and potholes. Evidence of the power of water to dissolve limestone is also seen above ground, with sink holes and areas of limestone pavement. The National Nature Reserve is over 1000 feet above sea level and includes both hard millstone grit and porous limestone. Moorland plants such as heather cover the millstone grit, while limestone provides a habitat for a variety of rare flowers, including autumn gentian and mossy saxifrage. This walk offers one route through the reserve but you are free to wander along the other paths and open moorland, exploring this magnificent upland reserve.

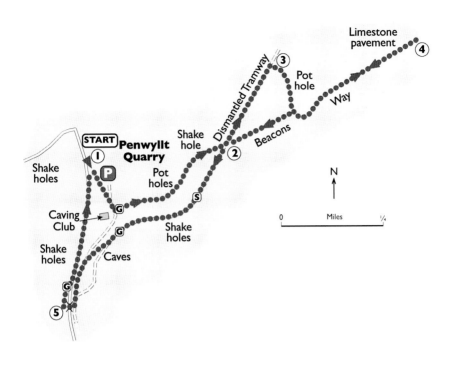

WALK 17

Penwyllt Quarry.

THE IRON AGE FORTS OF GARN GOCH

DESCRIPTION Exploration of one of the most significant Iron Age sites in Wales, with a circular tour of the woods and pasture surrounding the hill.

DISTANCE AND TERRAIN 3 miles. The route follows tracks, small paths and fields, as well as some quiet lanes. There are excellent views, but the paths are indistinct in places and some careful route-finding is needed across the fort and through field sections. May be wet in places but well worth these minor alerts!

START Small car park at the foot of Garn Goch, about 1m south of the hamlet of Bethlehem and about 3m from Llangadog. SN 682243.

DIRECTIONS From Bethlehem, follow the brown signs towards Heneb Garn-goch. About 1 mile from the village, turn left into a 'no through road'. Immediately cross a cattle grid and find the parking area on the left. An interpretation panel offers a good introduction to the site.

I Bethlehem is at the western end of the Beacons Way, a 95-mile long distance footpath that traverses the National Park. The first part of the walk follows this route over the Iron Age forts of Garn Goch. From the car park, walk up the obvious grass track at the back of the information panel. It curves up to the right heading for the main ridge through a glorious heath with bracken and rough pasture. Enjoy panoramic views across the Towy valley. The path soon crosses over the 'small' fort, 'Y Gaer Fach'. *Although the remains are intermittent, there is evidence of two sets of ramparts here.* A slight depression then leads on towards the main event, Y Gaer Fawr, or 'large' fort, climbing steeply up side of the hill. *There are various ways across or around the fort; the paths are indistinct and confusing. However, it doesn't really matter which tack you take as long as you reach the far side at Point 2.* To cross the main fort, watch out for a faint fork to the left as you climb up to the ramparts. Follow this left as it climbs the scree diagonally, leaving the main grass path to circumnavigate the stones. A small but clear path then goes across the centre of the fort. The extensive views indicate the surveillance potential of this site. Pass just to the right of the highest stony tump and then head down on a faint path into a shallow depression. At the far side of this dip, trend right. Your route is soon confirmed as it becomes a broad path heading downhill to the right and soon meeting a road.

2 Turn right and follow the small road until it comes to a gate. Continue through the gate towards Garn-wen. The road becomes a farm access track, but, within 100 yards, leave this to bear left through a gate, signed with a Beacons Way marker. Follow thispath, bordered by hedges with oak and silver birch trees, to join a green lane. It may be wet in places but dries out as it begins to ascend. At a T-junction with another track, turn right to stay on the Beacons Way. A good stony track slants diagonally up the hillside, with the ridge of Pen y Bicws striding above you on the left. In just over ¼ mile, reach a fingerpost at Bwlch y Gors. *The terrain lives up to its name, 'the marshy pass'.*

3 Turn right to leave the main track here. Follow a Beacons Way sign over a short boggy area, soon crossing a stile. Pass through another gateway and then go around the edge of a field to reach another stile on the edge of the woods. The landscape now changes to woodland and the path starts level before turning right and descending to a T-junction with a track.

4 Turn right, go through a gate and then turn immediately left, crossing a stile. The path continues down the edge of a wood, squelchy in places. When the trees end, maintain the same direction, crossing fields. Approaching a cottage, go to the left of it and pass through a gate to reach the road.

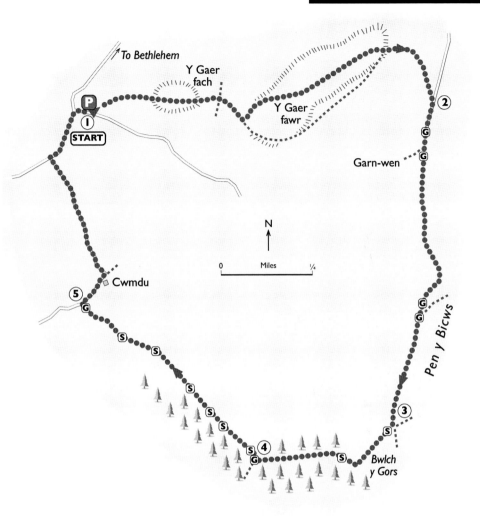

5 Turn right to follow the quiet road. In 200 yards, turn right and continue to follow the lane for another ¼ mile, then bending to the right. Follow the road back to the starting point.

Garn Goch

Garn Goch is one of the most impressive Iron Age sites in Wales. There were two forts straddling the strategic hill. The large fort is over 200m above sea level and commands extensive views across the Towy Valley, a key route through western Wales. The site will have been home to a busy farming community around 2000 years ago. There is still evidence on the ground, with the remains of stone ramparts and posterns (gateway sites).

THE MIGHTY FORTRESS OF CARREG CENNEN

DESCRIPTION The castle makes a dramatic and photogenic starting point and is in view for much of the walk. A gentle descent through oak woodland leads to a crossing of the River Cennen. The route then curves around the facing hillside through porous limestone country, before re-crossing the river and climbing back up to the mighty fortress on its rocky bluff. This route is one of the waymarked routes from Carreg Cennen Castle and is signed with red 'castle' markers. Yellow markers indicate a shorter route between points 2 and 4.

DISTANCE AND TERRAIN 4½ miles. Hilly circuit with some steep sections.

START Start at the car park for the castle, SN 666194. The car park closes at 16.00 in winter and 18.30 in summer.

1 Go through the gate, and pass the café. *This also has an information point and gift shop; it's a great place to start or finish your walk with fantastic views across the surrounding countryside.* Climb the path heading directly towards the castle, which is also the Beacons Way. It veers left below the rocky bluff and comes to the castle entrance. *To explore the majestic remains of this Norman landmark, turn right here, paying your entrance fee to Cadw at the ticket hut – or visit at the end of your walk. This is a commanding vantage point. An information panel points out the escarpment of the Black Mountain, with the Bronze Age burial cairns, Tair Uchaf and Tair Isaf, silhouetted on the skyline.* The main walk goes straight ahead through a gate. A lovely path slants downhill through the oak wood of Coed Cennen. Reach the River Cennen at the bottom of the valley.

2 (At this point the shorter yellow castle trail doubles back, continuing along the river bank on a level course. It re-joins this walk at Point 4.) Cross the footbridge, following the red castle waymarks. Soon cross another footbridge and continue uphill through woodland on a broad path. Cross a stile to a farm track crossing. At this point, bear half left and take the track zigzagging uphill. It almost immediately bends sharp right and a little way further on, bends back to the left. On this left hand bend, keep straight ahead on to another track, but staying on the Beacons Way and following the red waymarks. *As you climb, there are increasingly good views across the valley of Castle Cennen, perched on its dramatic limestone crag. Take time to trace the route you've taken so far.* Reaching the top, continue on a path across fields, then curving to the left. Join a track and pass the barns and farm at Brondei to reach a road.

3 Turn right and follow the quiet road through a small valley, crossing a cattle grid. In about ¼ mile, turn right to follow a footpath over a stile and across a field. The path turns sharp left around a deep shake hole and continues through a field. It soon becomes a track, descending gently through delightful and picturesque limestone scenery alongside the river. Take care here. Pass through a marshy area and weave your way across the fields until you come to a T-junction with a track. Turn right here, heading downhill. Cross a cattle grid, ford the stream and then keep on the track.

4 As the track comes to a fork at the house of Llwyn bedw, bear left to leave the track. The path descends the field, and it's steep! *Across the valley looms the imposing buttress of Castle Carreg Cennen.* Cross the footbridge and climb the bank to the road.

5 Turn left walking up the road for about 300 yards. Watch for a fingerpost indicating a footpath across the field. Go through the gate and follow this path, aiming for the buildings below the castle. This brings you to the door of the café and the track back to the car park.

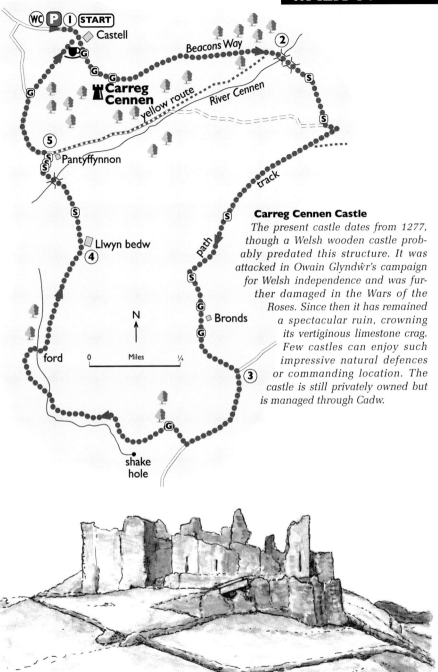

Carreg Cennen Castle

The present castle dates from 1277, though a Welsh wooden castle probably predated this structure. It was attacked in Owain Glyndŵr's campaign for Welsh independence and was further damaged in the Wars of the Roses. Since then it has remained a spectacular ruin, crowning its vertiginous limestone crag. Few castles can enjoy such impressive natural defences or commanding location. The castle is still privately owned but is managed through Cadw.

Carreg Cennen Castle

USK RESERVOIR

DESCRIPTION Most reservoirs have a path or trail around them, but Usk Reservoir is rather special. Its location is particularly picturesque and tranquil, high in the remote and wild foothills of the Black Mountains, with tantalising glimpses of the mountains through the trees. This circuit of the 280 acre reservoir uses the waymarked cycle and walking loop. It is easy to follow and offers a variety of excellent views of forest, lake and the surrounding stark moorlands.

DISTANCE AND TERRAIN 6 miles. Stone dressed forest roads with easy gradients.

START Forestry car park at Pont ar Wysg, on the road between Trecastle and Llanddeusant. SN 820272. The walk could equally well be started from the car park by the reservoir dam at Point 3 on the map, SN 834286.

DIRECTIONS The village of Trecastle is situated about midway between Brecon and Llandovery on the A40. From here, take the road towards Llanddeusant, following this for about 5 miles. At the far end of Glasfynydd Forest there is a car park on the left, immediately before Pont ar Wysg.

Pont ar Wysg is the first bridge on the River Usk. It takes the mountain road between Llanddeusant and Trecastle across the infant river about 3 miles north of its source on the boggy slopes of the Black Mountain. There is a grand panorama of the photogenic profile of the rugged escarpment of Fan Brycheiniog south from here. To the north, the high ridge of Mynydd Myddfai rises above the forests of the Usk reservoir. The Roman road from Brecon to Llandovery crossed the nape of this ridge with evidence of marching camps at Y Pigwn and a fortlet at nearby Waun Ddu. Older cairns and remains are dotted across the wild moorland.

I Take the track opposite the car park, marked as a cycle track and leading gently downhill into the forest. In 300m keep straight ahead at a junction. Weave left over a hillock and then down to cross the River Usk, still; a stream, here. Curve to the right on the other side and then soon bend sharp left, to go around the south western spur of the reservoir.

2 Soon after the western extremity of the water, follow the cycleway and trail to the right Soon after passing the end of the reservoir, the track keeps close or near to the north shore for 1½ miles to the intake works. Soon after this the track curves to the right to follow the water's edge. About ½ mile further, arrive at the end of the reservoir dam. Turn right to cross the dam, reaching the car park on the far side. You could equally well start the walk here.

3 Turn right and follow the road for about ½ mile, at first alongside the reservoir and then veering south and leaving the shore. Ignore a road turning off sharp right, but watch out for another junction about 300m yards further on.

4 Turn right here to leave the road but to stay on the reservoir trail along a forest road. Follow this as it meanders around the forest, later bending left and then right, to reach the outward route. At the junction, turn left to walk the short distance back to Pont ar Wysg.

River Usk

The Usk is the third longest river entirely in Wales, rising on the slopes of the Black Mountain and travelling over 60 miles before its confluence with the Severn Estuary south of Newport. The Usk valley is a key route into the heartland of Wales and has been used by the Romans, drovers, and the modern day A40. Its headwaters were captured in 1955 by building a dam. The resulting 280 acre Usk reservoir was designed to provide drinking water for Swansea but is also a popular spot for fishermen and a prime site for catching trout. Its remote location, over 1000 feet above sea level, has been designated as a dark sky site.

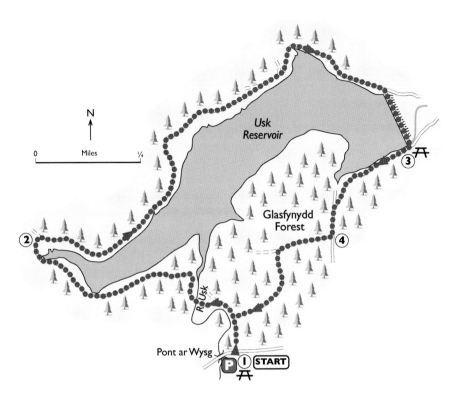

Usk Reservoir

PRONUNCIATION

Welsh	English equivalent
c	always hard, as in **c**at
ch	as in the Scottish word lo**ch**
dd	as th in **th**en
f	as f in o**f**
ff	as ff in o**ff**
g	always hard as in **g**ot
ll	no real equivalent. It is like 'th' in then, but with an 'L' sound added to it, giving 'thlan' for the pronunciation of the Welsh 'Llan'.

In Welsh the accent usually falls on the last-but-one syllable of a word.

KEY TO THE MAPS

Main road

Minor road

Route

① Walk instruction

– – – Adjoining path

Stream

Ⓖ Gate

Ⓢ Stile

△ Summit

Woods

Pub

Ⓟ Parking

THE COUNTRYSIDE CODE

• Be safe – plan ahead and follow any signs

• Leave gates and property as you find them

• Protect plants and animals, and take your litter home

• Keep dogs under close control

• Consider other people

Open Access
Some routes cross areas of land where walkers have the legal right of access under The CRoW Act 2000 introduced in May 2005. Access can be subject to restrictions and closure for land management or safety reasons for up to 28 days a year. Details from: www.naturalresourceswales.gov.uk.
Please respect any notices.

Published by **Kittiwake-Books Limited**
3 Glantwymyn Village Workshops, Glantwymyn, Machynlleth, Montgomeryshire SY20 8LY

© Text & map research: Alastair Ross 2016
© Maps & illustrations: Kittiwake-Books Ltd 2016
Drawings by Morag Perrott
Cover photos: Main: Pen y Fan *Inset:* Carreg Cennen Castle. *Supplied by www.alamy.com*

Care has been taken to be accurate. However neither the author nor the publisher can accept responsibility for any errors which may appear, or their consequences. If you are in any doubt about access, check before you proceed.

Printed by Mixam UK.

ISBN: **978 1 908748 36 2**